Survival Guide
—— for the ——
Not-for-Profit Board Member

governance
guru

*practical
governance*
SERIES

PRACTICAL GOVERNANCE

Survival Guide
for the
Not-for-Profit Board Member

Debi J. Peverill

Copyright ©2024 Debi J. Peverill

Published by Painless Financial Training Group Inc
5 Florence Street,

Lower Sackville, Nova Scotia

Canada B4J 1C5

Reproduction of this material in whole or in part without written authorization, by any duplication process whatsoever, both present and future, is a violation of copyright and offenders risk prosecution.

Disclaimer: Nothing in this book is intended to replace advice that is specific to your circumstances. This book is for educational purposes and is not professional advice.

ISBN: 978-1-989228-21-0 (paperback)
ISBN: 978-1-989228-22-7 (e-book)

Survival Guide
for the
Not-for-Profit
Board Member

CONTENTS

Chapter One: Governance in General.......... 1
About Governance *1*
Governance Is Everywhere *4*
Why I Care about Governance....................... *6*
Why You Should Care about Governance *7*
Specific Things That Could Go Wrong *9*
Public Trust...................................... *10*
Stakeholders..................................... *13*
Governance Table................................. *17*

Chapter Two: Duty of Care 19
Due Diligence and Negligence *21*
ADAPPT = The Board Decision-Making Framework...... *25*

Chapter Three: Duty of Skill 31
Liability... *32*
Other Skills...................................... *34*

Chapter Four: Duty of Knowledge 37
Law under Which the Organization Was Incorporated *38*
Other Laws....................................... *39*
Regulations...................................... *39*
Bylaws of the Organization *40*
Policies and Procedures............................ *41*
Conflict of Interest *41*
Confidentiality.................................... *42*

Chapter Five: Duty of Loyalty 43

Chapter Six: Fiduciary Duty.................. 45
Fiduciary Duty *46*
Budgets... *47*
Internal Control *48*
Tax Issues....................................... *51*
Funding Agreements.............................. *52*

Chapter Seven: Duty of Management 53
Understand the Board Member's Role. 53
Balancing the Roles 56
Attendance. 58
Board Discipline 59

Chapter Eight: Directors' Rights 61
Ability to Vote. 61
Access to Management 63
Access to Governance Documents. 64

Chapter Nine: Board Training 65

Chapter Ten: Insurance. 69

Chapter Eleven: To Summarize ... Staying Out of Trouble. 73
Protection for Board Members. 73
Characteristics of Board Members. 76

Glossary. 81

Other Books by Debi J. Peverill 85

About the Author. 87

For More Information. 89

CHAPTER ONE
Governance in General

Clare Booth Luce once said that no good deed goes unpunished. Volunteer organizations are a prime example of this. Organizations are formed with good intentions of achieving important goals. If you want to achieve the goal of the group, you need more than good intentions. You need to understand what could go wrong and how to avoid problems. In short, you need governance.

This is not a book about how you should be a good citizen and donate your time to a board. This is a book about all the things that could go wrong, what your responsibilities are, and how you can prevent bad things from happening. Bad things could happen, but if you read this book, they won't happen to you.

ABOUT GOVERNANCE

Are you a board member of a not-for-profit organization? Are you concerned about whether you are liable for the activities of the organization? If so, you have come to the right place.

This book will prepare you for your role as the director of a not-for-profit organization. You may not have heard the term governance before; in fact, sometimes when I tell people that I am a governance expert, they assume I work for the government.

I like to say that governance is the glue that holds civilization together. What makes a driver stop their car at a red light? The Motor Vehicle Act and enforcement by the police department. That is governance. For the same reason, everyone in North America drives on the right-hand side of the road. Imagine if that was not the rule. That would be chaos, which is the opposite of good governance.

Governance is the web of laws, regulations, conventions, and enforcement that keeps our civilization working. How does this apply to board members? A board member takes the responsibility for the operations of a corporation, whether it is a business corporation or a not-for-profit organization.

As people, we are all responsible for our own actions once we are over the age of majority – eighteen years of age where I live. Children under the age of eighteen are their parents' responsibility; their parents have to pay for anything they mess up. This is a similar situation to that of the board member. Because a not-for-profit organization is not a "real person," others must accept responsibility for the actions of the organization. These others are referred to as directors or board members.

Governance in action is board members taking responsibility for the activities of an organization. This book is about the duties and responsibilities of board members.

There is a difference between being a member of an organization and being a board member.

When you are a member of an organization, you are not liable or responsible for anything that happens. If, however, you bow to pressure and allow your name to stand as a board member or director of the organization, then you have accepted more responsibility and more liability. These liabilities arise from the existence of laws that impose responsibilities on the board members to control the activities of the corporations or organizations.

Legislation that applies to organizations sets up board liability. These laws include responsibilities for payments of employee deductions, safety violations, environmental issues, sales taxes, privacy rules, and other compliance issues!

A board member should determine which of the laws applying to the organization have a provision for directors' liability. Then see whether the organization is compliant with the laws and, if not, discover how to bring the organization into compliance. Legislators come up with laws establishing directors' liability to get the attention of the organization and encourage them to be compliant.

Governance comprises all the policies and procedures for how everything actually works. It is the fabric that keeps civilization together. I have argued that everything is a governance issue. If there is a problem, then either a policy was missing or a policy was not followed. I have asked people to bring me any news story that they think is not a governance story, and I will explain to them why they are wrong. Governance is everywhere.

GOVERNANCE IS EVERYWHERE

I see governance everywhere. You have some governance in your families. Not too many families have procedure manuals, but that does not mean there are no rules. What is the procedure when you are going to be late for supper? How is the loading and unloading of the dishwasher handled? Are there any rules about the toilet seat being up or down? What if you use the last of the toilet paper in the bathroom? You can see there are procedures around all these policies. And this forms the governance framework in your home.

In my home, it used to be that my children were allowed to do whatever they wanted unless someone had told them they couldn't. One day when I returned to my home after work, I found that my son and his friends were using their skateboards to slide down the steps from the second floor to the first floor of our home. They had taken the wheels off their boards so they would slide better. I noted that the plasterboard at the bottom of the stairs was cracked from them repeatedly banging into it. When I asked him why they were doing such a thing, I got an answer I assume you have heard before. "Well, no one ever told us not to!" So I changed the governance structure in our home that day from the *You can do whatever you want unless you have been told not to*, to the more useful *You are not allowed to do anything ever unless one of your parents has told you it is okay*.

This changed the model to one where everything is forbidden unless permission is granted. The benefit of this change was that I did not have to try to think of all the things a kid might do that I should forbid. I would not have ever thought to forbid the removal of the wheels from the skateboard so it could be turned into a vehicle for sliding down the stairs. It takes a lot of imagination to try and dream up a list of things you do not want people to do.

When we consider policies, it is a best practice to explain the reasoning for a policy. For example, I might have said something like, *You are not allowed to do anything where you might get hurt.* But that could preclude one from simply walking up or down stairs. You need to further refine the policy. What about forbidding anything where the chance of getting hurt is higher than 30 percent. One would then need a matrix of some sort to enable the kid to estimate their chances of getting hurt.

My more responsible child participated in jumping off the roof of our house. No one was hurt because, at the time, the yard had about ten feet of snow. This would suggest a flexible policy: *You can only jump off the roof when there is sufficient snow to break your fall.* How does this apply in your organization?

Designing governance strategies is not for the faint of heart. There needs to be a fair amount of thought and discussion. The benefit of a well-designed governance structure is that is should be set up in such a way that most activities are covered by the policies, and that the employees, or children in my example, feel like they are being trusted to make their own choices. Allowing the stakeholders to make their own decisions should lead to better control over dangerous activities, in my example anyway.

WHY I CARE ABOUT GOVERNANCE

I have spent a couple of decades talking about governance. On occasion, a participant in one of my workshops will accuse me of being negative. I agree that the results of not paying attention to governance can be quite negative, but my goal is a positive one. I want people to know enough about governance that they are able to guide their organization to achieving all the organization's goals.

I focus mainly on not-for-profit organizations because

public companies have access to governance training provided by their corporations. Self-employed business owners do not have as much need for governance as they are dealing with their own money. They don't have to be careful; they aren't letting anyone down but themselves if they make the wrong decisions.

Board members of not-for-profit organizations are accepting responsibility for these organizations and need some assistance. This book is for them.

WHY YOU SHOULD CARE ABOUT GOVERNANCE

You should care about governance because it is governance principles that will protect you from personal liability.

One of the clearest examples of what could go wrong is when a board member is asked to pay a bill that is owed by the organization.

For example, in Canada, directors could be liable for items like source deductions. The Employment Insurance payments, Canada Pension Plan payments, and income tax withheld from employees is sent by the employer to the Canada Revenue Agency (CRA) the month after these payments are withheld. If the payments are not made, then CRA can ask the directors to do so using their personal funds, and this is a legal requirement. Therefore, if you are serving on a board and the source deductions are not being paid, it is possible you will be asked to pay these amounts personally. This is not a good organization for you to join, unless you wanted to send your money to CRA for a bill that is not even yours!

Board members need to ensure that the organization itself is paying all its bills. Of course, you need to understand financial matters enough that you can tell whether all the or bills are being paid. We will talk about how directors can protect themselves in chapter 9. What about being sued? If the board is being sued when you join the board, then the lawsuit is not your personal problem. You are only responsible for lawsuits that show up after you join the board. But as with the source deductions, an organization that is having legal trouble might be prone to doing things that cause them to be sued.

Legislators want the legislation they are passing to apply to everyone involved. They are not impressed with the idea that if it is the corporation has created this problem it will be the corporation that gets punished. Legislators generally like to get their hands on a real person. For all corporations, whether they are incorporated under the for-profit or the not-for-profit acts, the directors are the ones who are going to be held accountable for the actions of the corporation; they are liable.

As a volunteer on a board, you are donating your time because you have an interest in what is being done by this organization. You are there to help. You do not expect to become liable for any action that might be taken by the board. Governance training helps you to avoid making the kinds of mistakes that get volunteers into trouble.

SPECIFIC THINGS THAT COULD GO WRONG

Employment Matters

There are risks associated with having employees. The hiring and firing and discipline of employees can use up a bunch of committee and board time. Again, the way to reduce this risk is to hire experts to draft employment policies that comply with all the various federal and provincial legislations. Then actually follow your own policies. This should reduce the risk of catastrophic wrongful dismissal suits to a reasonable level.

Harassment or Assault

The news has been full of cases where the leadership of an organization has been criticized for their diligence in reacting to allegation of harassment or assault. Every organization must have policies to allow victims to report their allegations and get meaningful assistance from the organization. There are laws, and the organization should get expert advice to ensure they remain compliant with these laws. Keep in mind that mere compliance is a lower standard than having ethical behaviour. Most of us aspire to behaving better than simply avoiding breaking the law.

Environmental Issues

There are risks that exist when the organization owns property. The owner of land is the person responsible for anything that happens on that land. For example, if an oil spill contaminates land, it has to be "remediated," which costs money, often a lot of money. If the insurance for the organization is not sufficient to pay for the remediation, then the department of environment will probably levy a fine. The fine may have to be paid by the directors if the organization cannot raise the funds.

Health and Safety

Does your group hold events? If so, there are rules, many rules about what has to happen at these events to ensure the safety of the participants. Someone on your board or in management should have a working knowledge of the relevant health and safety legislation in your area.

Experts may be needed to develop policies and interpret all the rules that will need to be followed. At a minimum, the organization needs to develop a safety plan for the event.

PUBLIC TRUST

Public engagement and trust are necessary when you are trying to promote a cause or to raise money. You need to have the public believe in your organization and its purpose in order to achieve your organization's goals. However, public trust takes a long time to build up and can be lost in a moment.

Years ago, the Tylenol brand faced a loss of public trust. Somehow a bad actor was able to tamper with the packaging of the Tylenol painkiller, and people who took the pills died. Tylenol faced the loss of their credibility, lawsuits, and an existential crisis. The board and management swung into action. They took responsibility immediately for the problem, they figured out how it happened, and they informed the public. They took care of the families of the people who were killed, and then they came up with tamper-proof packaging.

Over time, Tylenol has gained back the trust they lost during that crisis.

Others have followed this method of dealing with negative publicity. Here in Canada, Maple Leaf Foods had a similar problem. Some of their products were tainted with listeria, a bacteria that can make people sick or even die. Maple Leaf Foods followed the Tylenol game plan. They got in front of the news cycle by telling everyone that they would find out what had happened, that they had closed plants, taken the products off the market, and they would be compensating anyone who was affected by this issue. The president of Maple Leaf Foods – one of the McCain family – was the spokesperson for this, not a hired employee. He showed up to press conferences and told the truth.

Compare this strategy with the baseball players refusing to admit that they took steroids. We still hear about Roger Clemons, who is widely believed to have used steroids to improve his performance (teammates have clearly said he took steroids). He still adamantly refuses to admit this. So, it is still news. Reporters are always hoping that one day he will change his story, and that they will be there to record it.

Public trust is based on doing the right thing – the ethical thing. And this trust has to be earned. A new organization will be met with some skepticism until it has demonstrated that the group is committed to working with the community in an ethical manner.

Repeated scandals of people in power behaving in an unethical manner damage all of us, because this type of news lowers the publics trust in anyone. I know there are people who think that all board members serve on a board to get something for themselves, to benefit monetarily from this service. For volunteers, it can be particularly annoying to have people suspect your motives when all you are doing is trying to help, and you are doing it for free.

People see a board as a group of people sitting around a table taking care of themselves first and then taking care of their friends. There are those who will never be convinced otherwise.

Edelman publishes the results of a survey each year – Edelman Trust Barometer – showing the level of public trust demonstrated by groups who fill in a questionnaire. Several years ago, Canadians fell below 50 percent for the first time. This means that fewer than half of Canadians trust business, government, or other institutions.

It is against this backdrop that people choose to serve on a board, knowing that half of the people they meet will question their reasons for serving. That can be very upsetting when the motive for serving is to give back to a community and try to make a difference.

STAKEHOLDERS

A stakeholder is a person who has an interest in an organization — employees, shareholders, suppliers, customers, or the general public.

The general public is the stakeholder that is occasionally a surprise to board members. The general public will feel they have a stake in any organization that receives public funding. Therefore, if your group receives public funding – the group could receive close scrutiny.

As an organization, take a few minutes and make a list of all the possible stakeholders. Then look at how you serve these stakeholders. There should be something written beside each stakeholder category explaining how they are served by the organization.

Employees

The employees of the not-for-profit organization are the actual people who implement the decisions made by the board. Problems arise when the board is not doing a good job of coming up with practical guidance.

The employees are most likely to be the face of the organization, and it is important for the board to have policies that keep these stakeholders happy.

Employees are also impacted by the behaviour of the executive director. If the board only interacts with the executive director, and they are not being fair to the employees, then the board may not hear about this. A prudent board considers a process for the employees to have access to a human resources committee member. Tread carefully here: you do not want the employees to see a way to go over the head of the executive director with any frivolous complaints. You also want to be sure the employees know they can reach out to someone other than the executive director if there is something that needs to be addressed.

General Public

If you are receiving government money, the general public will feel, with some justification, that you should be telling them what you are doing with this money. A process for making your activities public will be needed. Websites, annual meetings, or social media can all be used to let people know what you are up to.

If your group serves the public, then you can be sure some people will not be pleased with how you do that and will complain. Your organization needs a privacy officer and maybe a complaints officer as well. There has to be a process for any member of the public to make a complaint.

Considering the public is important when making plans that will affect them. Public meetings are a popular choice to explain what is happening and to give the public a chance to ask their questions.

Members

The board is elected by the members, and it is key to listen to what they want. Charities are an example of mission-driven organizations; sports organizations tend to be member driven.

The members have their chance to talk at the annual general meeting. After that, they leave the running of the organization to the board. This does not mean you should ignore the members until the next election.

Member surveys are an excellent way to see what the members want and don't want. If you want to be re-elected, it is a good idea to brag about the good work you are doing on behalf of the members.

Figure out how the board can serve the members and make it so.

Funders

For a not-for-profit organization, a funder is a person or a group who provides money to the organization. These stakeholders are very important to the organization because without funding the organization cannot achieve their goals.

Most funders will be quite willing to tell you what they want, but there is still some benefit in figuring out what you can offer and making an approach to a new funder, or to a current funder for additional funding.

Board Members or Directors

Your board members are also stakeholders of course. For volunteer boards, some form of volunteer appreciation is needed.

A wise organization will make sure that the board members feel their efforts are being appreciated. Typical events are a volunteer appreciation dinner or awards for volunteer of the year. You can also provide items like T-shirts and coffee mugs. You cannot actually pay a volunteer or give them significant gifts that could be interpreted as remuneration. The joke that meetings should be held in warm places in the winter is not appropriate.

Trust Intermediaries or Influencers

Here is a stuck-up type of word. Trust intermediaries are a group of your supporters who are not employees, board members, or funders, but who say nice things about you on social media. You have impressed these people. Figuring out what they need to hear from you in order to continue to support the group is important.

For example, it might be good to send out advance notifications about coming events to your trust intermediaries. They can get the buzz started ahead of time and hopefully make the event a larger success.

GOVERNANCE TABLE

So, what are the responsibilities of a board member? I'll be talking about duties of care, skill, knowledge, loyalty; about fiduciary duty; and about duty of management. I'll also talk about the rights of a board member, how to stay out of trouble, board training, and finally insurance.

I have put a table together that shows what we are going to talk about in this book: the duties and reponsibilities, what the goals are, and how you can accomplish them. This gives you an overview.

Duty	Goals	Responsi-bilities	Rights	Tasks
Duty of Care	Act in a reasonable manner. Be accountable for the organization's affairs. Make sure activities are transparent.	Maintain confidentiality.	Be given notice of meetings and allowed to vote at meetings.	Read meeting packages, attend meetings, and voice your opinion.
Duty of Skill	Plan for succession and diversity.	Obtain necessary training and professional advice where appropriate.	Be given notice of meetings and allowed to vote at meetings.	Use all your skills.
Duty of Knowledge	Avoid conflict of interest.	Understand the operations of the board.	Be given notice of meetings and allowed to vote at meetings.	Attend training sessions.
Duty of Loyalty	Be supportive of the organization (only disagree at the meeting during the discussion).	Maintain confidentiality.	Be given notice of meetings and allowed to vote at meetings.	
Fiduciary Duty	Implementation of assessment and control procedures.	Understand financial matters.	Be given access to financial records.	Review budgets and other financial information.
Duty of Management	Establish strategic direction, mission, vision, and values.	Commit to staff of the organization.		

CHAPTER TWO
Duty of Care

The duty of care is the most important duty a director will need to concern themselves with. This duty is the one that could lead to being personally responsible for actions or non-actions taken by the board.

Stated simply, board members have a responsibility to act in the best interests of the organization and must behave in a way such that a reasonable person would behave. The reasonable person test is generally applied by others, and it is usually applied in hindsight.

Applying the test later means that documentation must be kept that will show the board has acted in a reasonable way. This type of documentation can go beyond the minutes, but the minutes should show the motions that were made, the discussion that took place, and the experts who were consulted, if any, before a decision was made.

For example, remember the story of Kyle Beach, a player who was allegedly abused by a coach working for the Chicago Black Hawks. In 2010, he reported these events to all the appropriate parties: the coach, the general manager, and the union for the hockey players. It appears that no one took action, despite clear policies to the contrary. The people who failed to act were asked to resign from their positions, eleven years later. This is the duty of care in action. These people did not act as a reasonable person would be expected to behave.

The minutes of a meeting where the matter was discussed have proved pivotal in the current investigation, and people who attended this meeting, or had knowledge about it, are the ones who are being disciplined.

These people are being judged more than a decade after the events took place, which means we are seeing sexual abuse through a different lens than was in place in 2010. This type of example should frighten others into making sure they are exercising their duty of care and acting in a reasonable manner.

The changing of public perceptions over time can be problematic. Sexual abuse was not tolerated in 2010, but there are other examples. When I attended university in the 1970s, we were allowed to smoke in class. Our professors smoked in some cases. One of the university buildings I spent time in had a grey haze in a few of the windowless classrooms. This type of behaviour was considered reasonable at the time. Now, it's disgusting. Indoor smoking is prohibited everywhere. The universities have a smoke-free campus. Smoking in class now would be illegal.

The climate at the time a decision is made will be

considered, but it is hard to look back at some decisions and imagine how this was permitted. A board member who is aware of their duty of care should be thinking about how the decisions will look in ten years.

DUE DILIGENCE AND NEGLIGENCE

To satisfy your duty of care, you must show that a reasonable person would have made the same decision. You do this by demonstrating due diligence. Due diligence is often explained as the absence of negligence and negligence is explained as the absence of due diligence so the entire definition circles back to how a reasonable person would behave.

Due Diligence

For example, a sign says THIN ICE. If board members see this sign and then decide to carry on skating, then most of us would agree they have been negligent. They were warned, and they have chosen to ignore this warning. If a board member falls into the water, then negligence will be easy to prove.

How could the board defend itself from this charge of negligence? Is the sign a credible warning? Could they argue that the sign was from last year, or had been up for two weeks and the weather had been very cold and therefore the ice was no longer thin. Could they have taken safety precautions such as roping together and wearing life preservers to mitigate the risk. Could they have called in their own experts? You see the trend here. Did the board have a credible reason for deciding the sign was not relevant to their decision? Lots of questions here, and some of them could be asked to see whether a board was negligent.

The board can demonstrate due diligence by considering all the facts before they make any decision. It can also be helpful for the board to consult with experts. If there is a legal decision, then asking a lawyer would be the best practice.

However, if no one falls in the water, then there is "no harm, no foul" with no consequences. The board may not find themselves being disciplined for every case in which they were negligent.

Negligence

A board can be sued for negligence if something goes very wrong because of one of their decisions. If a board member is acting in an honest manner with a view to the best interests of the organization, there should be no problem with being found to be negligent.

Some board members worry too much about some of these possibilities. And, of course, some boards do not think about these issues at all.

POLICIES

Policies can improve your chances of not being negligent. Put some time into establishing the correct policies, and then just follow your policy. We talked in the first chapter about the benefits of explaining the purpose for a policy to stakeholders – they are more likely to follow the policy if they understand the reason for it.

You might avoid the issue of malicious compliance with some explanation. When people feel the policies have no purpose, they might follow the letter of the policy while undermining the purpose of the policy. For example, the boss who says, "Don't disturb me for the next hour no matter what," runs the risk of not being told that the building is on fire. If instead she said, "I need some time to work on this proposal undisturbed," then the employees who find out the building is burning are more likely to let her know. They have been trusted to follow their own instincts about when to interrupt the boss and when not to.

If the principle behind the policies is explained, then it is more likely that the intent of the policy will be achieved and you don't have to be so specific in the policy.

Your policies will evolve over time. For example, in 2019, I don't think too many groups had a pandemic policy. In an earlier book I wrote on governance, pandemics got one line in the policy section where I suggested the group have a policy about when employees would stop coming to work. Billions of words have been written about pandemics and risks associated with them since then. The risk of pandemic is now on everyones radar.

Risk Assessment

A board is responsible for being prudent about the activities they take on. A fancy word for that is risk management. A risk assessment looks at all the possible things that could go wrong and assesses the ways to mitigate all these risks. These risks might include items such as the loss of funding, natural disasters such as fires, floods, earthquakes, or any of the threats from cyber security issues.

A board needs to be careful without being overly cautious or suspicious about what could go wrong. If you are acting in the best interests of the organization and being careful, then all should be well. Boards need to be prudent without being paranoid. No one predicts the future with any amount of accuracy, and some threats will go undetected until they actually happen.

We refer to a threat no one sees coming as a Black Swan. The COVID-19 pandemic has been characterized as a Black Swan. The board has the responsibility to watch out for all threats and to be as prepared as possible for any credible threat. Some of that preparation includes having insurance – very useful for mitigating the natural disaster section of the threat profile. Other times the board looks for preventions, for example, internal controls that make it more difficult for an employee to steal from the organization. Safety and environmental policies also require policies, procedures, and checklists.

ADAPPT = THE BOARD DECISION-MAKING FRAMEWORK

Years ago, I developed a framework for boards to follow when making decisions. This framework is designed to help boards satisfy their duty of care and thus stay out of trouble. The duty of care requires board members to behave in an ethical manner with a view to the best interests of the organization. This framework works for any decision. The framework has the following aspects:

A = authority
D = diligence
A = accountability
P = policies
P = prudence
T = transparency

Authority

This is the first step in the decision-making process. If you do not have the authority to make the decision, then you do not need to deal with the rest of the framework, because you are not going to be making the decision.

A clear example of this occurred during the pandemic. All over the world, public health authorities have closed businesses and imposed rules on masking, capacity limits, and vaccination rules. These rules took precedence over any decisions that individual boards could make. Organizations did not have the authority to open or meet because of the decisions made by the national or provincial health departments.

In these situations, the group is following the rules set by others.

The first step toward any decision being made at a group meeting is to determine whether the board does, in fact, have the authority to make the decision or not.

Diligence

Assuming the group can make the decision, the next step is to determine whether they have all the information they need to make an informed decision. Do they have all the facts they would like to have? Are there experts they would like to hear from, to help them make the decision?

The need for diligence means last-minute additions to the agenda are not a good idea. Making decisions in a hurry is not the best practice. Better decisions are made when the group has all the facts and time to consider all facets of a decision.

The meeting package should be read before the meeting so the board has time to consider all the information before the meeting. Once the board members have agreed that they have been diligent and are ready to decide, then the board can move on to the accountability stage.

Accountability

Is the group ready to accept the responsibility for making this decision? Typically, this occurs when the group has all the information they need and have considered it carefully. They are ready to move on to the next steps on the framework.

If further time is needed by one or more board members, then the decision is tabled until the next meeting.

The board could also decide to refer the decision to a committee, or back to management, for further analysis. This step of the decision-making process is not over until the board is ready to move on.

Policies

Policies help to make decisions consistent and save the board time.

- Do you have a policy about this decision?
- Should you have a policy about this decision?
- Do you have a policy that you do not want to follow?

DO YOU HAVE A POLICY?

If the board has a policy on a topic, the chair can simply remind the board of the policy when the topic arises at a board meeting. You don't need to discuss the item again. The decision has effectively been made, provided you are comfortable following the policy.

SHOULD YOU HAVE A POLICY?

Is this the type of decision you might make again? Has this come up before? Board time is precious, so if this is a decision that might come up more than once, setting a policy will be a time saver and will help future iterations of the board.

Having a policy will also lead to the decisions being made more consistently – always an improvement in meeting performance.

DO YOU HAVE A POLICY THAT YOU DO NOT WANT TO FOLLOW?

Sometimes, the group has a policy but is reluctant to apply it. The duty of care requires members to act in the best interest of the organization. Making a decision against their own policies is a tough one to defend.

First, decide whether the policy in existence needs to be changed. Perhaps the policy was set a long time ago?

If the policy still seems relevant but the group does not want to follow it – figure out why. Is this situation a logical exception to the policy or is the group being illogical? For example, you may have a policy that you don't want to apply because it involves a friend of the board. This, of course, is wrong.

If you follow tennis, you may have seen Novak Djokovic being ejected from the US Open because he hit an official with a ball. The policy is clear and applies to everyone, but you can see the temptation. Novak was the number one seed, and forcing him to leave the tournament would reduce the number of viewers. Congratulations to the officials for correctly applying the policy, no matter who was involved.

Prudence

This only applies to not-for-profit situations. A not-for-profit board must use prudence when making decisions because they are not dealing with their own money. If their stakeholders include government funders, they should be especially careful to understand the terms of the funding agreement in assessing their risks.

A business is not required to be prudent, especially if all the board members are also shareholders. The group can decide whether prudence should be a part of their framework or not.

Transparency

One of the principles of good governance is transparency, that is, the board must be able to explain how and why decisions are made.

For example, the board is hiring a new executive director:

- They have an application form and a list of desirable qualities and characteristics.

- They advertise this position on both social media and conventional channels.
- A committee is struck to evaluate all the applications received and to score them on the qualities the board is looking for.
- The top ten highest-scoring candidates are interviewed by the committee, and the number of candidates is reduced to five.
- The five are interviewed again, and the list is further reduced to two.
- The full board interviews the final two and decides who will be hired.
- The board announces the candidate who is hired.
- In recording the minutes of the meeting in which the candidate was hired, only the name would be in the minutes and the synopsis of the process followed.

This is a transparent process. If necessary, the application form and the list of qualities and qualifications can be shown to anyone who asks. Transparency and privacy are competing principles on occasion. We should make the process transparent while keeping the participants private.

Actions that must not happen:

- The board releases the names of the applicants who were not successful.
- The board releases all the scores of the candidates.

CHAPTER THREE
Duty of Skill

What is the duty of skill? This means that you bring your professional skills to the boardroom table, for example, the type of skill that is demonstrated by someone with a designation. A Chartered Professional Accountant, a medical doctor, a lawyer, or a professional engineer. These people have deep subject matter expertise, and they are expected to use it on behalf of the organization when they serve on a board.

When I do governance training with lawyers in the audience, they are often disappointed that they have to use their legal skills while on the board. They don't want to be legally responsible, but a lawyer is always a lawyer and is expected to bring all their skills to a meeting.

As a Chartered Professional Accountant, I am expected to understand the financial statements and the budgets that are a big part of due diligence exercised by board members. Even in the situations where I am serving on the board as communication chair or the membership co-ordinator, I am still a professional accountant. This is unfortunate, as my presence on the board has been known to intimidate the treasurer.

I have been in the unhappy situation of having to say that there is something wrong with the numbers I am looking at, when the treasurer has not noticed anything amiss. Financial statements talk to me – it's a by-product of forty years of professional practice. It is my duty as a board member to point out any issues. I cannot ignore my expertise, even if doing so would make the meeting more pleasant and shorter. This is the duty of skill. If you have the skill and you do not use it, you will be criticized and you may be considered negligent.

LIABILITY

As a Chartered Professional Accountant, I also face a higher level of liability if I am serving on a board and there is something wrong with the finances of the organization.

For example, I have a greater responsibility to double check on something like source deductions than other board members. Source deductions are the money for Employment Insurance, Canada Pension Plan, and income tax that are withheld from employees and sent in to Canada Revenue Agency each month. The board can be personally liable for these payments if the organization does not do so.

Because of the directors' inherent personal liability,

many boards have a standard agenda item prompting them to ask management whether these source payments have been made. For any board member who is not a financial professional, asking the question and getting the answer satisfies their due diligence obligation. Because I am a CPA, I am held to a higher standard. What if management says that all the source deductions have been made, but I notice that the current liabilities on the balance sheet are continuing to rise? This could be happening because the source deductions are not being made. I must then ask for proof of the payments. I need to see the documentation from Canada Revenue Agency that shows that they have received the monthly payments.

If I do not take this additional step to make sure the payments are being made, then it is possible that I, myself, would have to pay the source deductions because I do not meet the due diligence test. It is a stronger test for me as a Chartered Professional Accountant than it is for people who do not have a financial designation.

When I serve on a board, I carry my own liability insurance. My professional liability insurance – that I am required to carry to keep my licence to practice – has a rider for each organization whose board I am serving on. I pay extra for this coverage and I think it is worth it.

OTHER SKILLS

What skills are you bringing to the boardroom table?

If you are new to a board, this could be your skill: being new. You might ask the question that needs to be asked about why things are done the way they are. I love it when a new person asks us something and the only answer any of us have is that we have always done it that way. Here is an opportunity to make a change to our procedures that we may not have noticed on our own.

I had a weird experience not long ago. I was getting new glasses, and the very young technician was asking me about how much time I spend each day looking at screens. I explained I was an accountant, a teacher, and a writer, and I did most of that on screens these days. He asked me what an accountant does. I was taken aback. I don't remember ever explaining what accounting was before. I stumbled through a few words about doing tax returns and helping people figure out whether they are making money or not, but I was not really satisfied with the explanation. This conversation was an example of the skill of being new!

Everyone who serves on a board brings their unique life experiences and viewpoints. You do not have to have a professional designation to be of use as a board member. The organization needs multiple points of view, which is one of the reasons a board of directors is needed and not just one board member.

An organization will often develop a skill matrix, which is a document showing all the skills that are needed on the board. Financial skills are often needed on a board. Everyone on the board needs to be able to read the financial statements and the budget, but you need a couple of board members who have expert financial knowledge. In addition, most boards will want to have some board members with legal expertise and will hire additional lawyers as needed. If an organization has employees, it will need someone with human resource experience. Hiring decisions and employee health and safety are also areas where board expertise will be needed.

The skill matrix comes into use when the board is considering succession. If you need to have a lawyer on the board at all times, and a current lawyer is leaving the board, then the nominating committee needs to be working on locating another lawyer to fill that spot on the board.

The board has other considerations when filling vacant positions. Diversity is a popular term and covers attributes such as gender, race, age, and disability. In general, a board will want to be as diverse as their stakeholders. If half of the stakeholders identify as women, then, in theory, half the board should also identify as women. The same criteria apply to race, age, and disability.

In Canada, the organizations that regulate public companies have focused their attention on gender equality on boards, but progress has been quite slow. My experience is that not-for-profit boards are more gender equal. This may be because most board people are not being paid to sit on the board of a not-for-profit organization. Board positions at not-for-profit organizations are often volunteer, whereas public companies pay their directors. In my experience, when people are being paid, more of them are men.

If the group is a not-for-profit group of professionals, then the board should also include some lay members. For example, the medical society of a province should include a few people who are not medical doctors. The medical doctors have all been trained in the same way, so all have similar biases. Having a couple of members on the board who think about issues in a different way than a medical doctor will be helpful for the organization. These lay members can explain how non-medical people would look at some of the decisions made by the group. That board might need to find financial experts, legal people, and some human resources people. A board of twelve people that contains ten doctors is not a very diverse board.

CHAPTER FOUR
Duty of Knowledge

What is the duty of knowledge? This is a board member's duty to understand enough about the organization and the organization's policies and procedures to be an effective board member. This extends beyond the policy manuals and requires a board member to read the meeting material that has been distributed prior to a meeting and to review the minutes of the meeting after it has been held.

Think of a situation where a board member has said, "I am sorry, I did not know that." This situation could have been avoided if the board member had paid attention to their duty of knowledge. For example, a board member could have disclosed a confidential matter to an outsider because this board member has not paid enough attention to the organization's policies to know about the confidentiality policy. What happens next depends on the board policy on breaking the rules.

Everyone and every organization are subject to a framework of governance that includes laws, regulations, policies, procedures, and best practices. There may also be ethics, codes of conduct, and licencing.

Some of these items carry more weight than others. This framework is in the rough order of relevance.

- law under which the organization was incorporated
- other laws that impact the operations of the organization, such as employment, health and safety, environmental, zoning, and so forth
- regulations of any laws that apply
- bylaws of the organization
- policies and procedures of the organization

LAW UNDER WHICH THE ORGANIZATION WAS INCORPORATED

If there is a law, that will take precedence over a policy, if the two documents do not agree. For example, if the law says you cannot enter a restaurant unless you have been double vaccinated, then it does not matter what the owner of the restaurant has for policies. A law will take precedence over a bylaw, and it is possible a federal law will override a provincial law. In Canada, there is a near-constant debate about who has responsibility for certain aspects of life: municipal, provincial, or federal government.

OTHER LAWS

The law where the organization was incorporated is the most important law. For example, some legislation prohibits a not-for-profit organization from owning property (land or buildings). Of course, anyone who has the money to buy property is allowed to buy property under typical property laws, but those laws will not apply to a not-for-profit organization whose incorporating documents prohibit land ownership. This would be a good thing for the board to understand as a part of their duty of knowledge.

Another incorporating document example is the ability to borrow money. There are not-for-profits organizations who are not allowed to borrow money.

Other laws that might apply include those concerning employment, environment, health, and so forth. The organization should ask their legal advisers for some direction about the laws that impact their operations. It is a board responsibility to make sure that they are aware of any governance framework changes and respond accordingly.

REGULATIONS

I remember when the HST (harmonized sales tax) was first introduced in Canada, some groups were slow to realize they had a responsibility to collect the tax or an opportunity to get refunds. A well-run organization has advisers that keep them up to date in these areas. Typically, professional accountants will let their clients know when tax laws change, and lawyers will give advice about new or changing laws. Most laws also have regulations, which are updated more frequently than the laws but will still cause trouble if the organization does not know about the changes.

The organization needs to let their advisers know they are being relied upon to provide this information and should not just assume that the lawyers are keeping them informed.

BYLAWS OF THE ORGANIZATION

The bylaws of the organization provide more details about basic rules, such as how many board members should be on the board at a time and whether there are any restrictions (e.g., geography) for choosing the members. The bylaws will also talk about quorum and such riveting matters as how long after the year end the annual general meeting must be held. Board members will need to be familiar with the bylaws as well. A bylaw cannot be changed unless 75 percent of the attendees at a general meeting agree to do so. Therefore, it is much harder to change a bylaw than it is to change a policy. A policy can be changed by a majority of board members. To change a bylaw, the organization needs to call a special meeting of the members and have 75 percent of them agree to the changes.

POLICIES AND PROCEDURES

Every group has some policies and procedures, and I have a book in this series about just that, covering the categories of policies that should be in place within the organization.

Wise groups will schedule some board training to help board members understand the policies.

Procedures come out of policies. The procedure shows how something is done. The policy usually lets you know the objective, but not always how you will achieve the objective – that is the role of the procedure. For example, the organization may have a policy that two people must authorize a payment. The procedure outlines how that happens. Either two people must sign the cheques, or two people must authorize the payment online. The procedure will also tell you where the cheques are kept or how to complete the online payment.

CONFLICT OF INTEREST

Every organization should have a policy on conflict of interest, and each board member should have a good understanding of what a conflict of interest is. A board member needs to understand that there are rules about participating in decisions at the boardroom table where there is some possibility of receiving a personal benefit.

A board member should read the agenda ahead of time, be aware of the topics coming up, and declare their conflict of interest prior to the meeting taking place.

CONFIDENTIALITY

Confidentiality is another policy that board members need to pay attention to. You do not want a board member divulging secrets to those who should not know them and then saying they did not know that something was confidential. These policies should be explained well and be confirmed in writing.

Things change and people forget. Items that were not confidential could become confidential. Board members personal or business lives can also change. They could now be involved in matters with an increased need for confidentiality.

Having an annual confirmation that the board members have read, understood, and agreed to follow both the confidentiality and the conflict of interest policies is necessary.

CHAPTER FIVE
Duty of Loyalty

The duty of loyalty requires a board member to be supportive of the organization at all times, except perhaps when around the boardroom table.

When a board member is speaking to anyone other than board members, they should not use derogatory language about the group. They should never say that they did not vote in favour of something that has been passed by the board. To all the outsiders, the board is a united front.

Dissent happens at the meeting, when the board is talking among themselves – this is where they disagree, respectfully of course. But once the board has voted, then the course of action is set, and the entire board is on the same team.

Board members will work hard to achieve the goals they set. If a board member voted against setting a goal, they are still going to work toward making the goal come true.

If a board decision does not work out, there is still no place for one of board members who voted against the passed motion to say I told you so. This is petty and unattractive. The board is on the same team.

The board will work to determine how they reached the wrong decision for the purposes of avoiding mistakes in the future, not to lay blame or point fingers.

A person who finds they are not agreeing with the others on the board should probably leave the board. It is possible that the vision of the organization does not align with the views of this board member.

When you are no longer on the board, the duties do not change. You are still not allowed to divulge matters that are confidential, nor are you permitted to air your grievance with the board. The duty of loyalty still applies.

CHAPTER SIX
Fiduciary Duty

A board has a duty to spend the money entrusted to them in a responsible manner. This is similar to the duty of care: what a reasonable person would do is also relevant here.

As a board member of a not-for-profit organization, you are not dealing with your own money. Therefore, a higher standard of care is necessary compared to when you are deciding how to spend your own paycheque.

If you think it would be a good idea to go to the casino with the money you raised at the monthly dinner and see whether you could double the money playing roulette, then you do not have the correct temperament to sit on a not-for-profit board. Boards must spend money wisely and be prepared to explain to their stakeholders exactly how they spent the money.

FIDUCIARY DUTY

What is fiduciary duty? Fiduciary is a word that means taking care of money.

The board must use the money they were entrusted with in a financially prudent manner. If they do not use the funds in a manner approved by the stakeholders, then these same stakeholders might sue them for breaching their fiduciary duty.

The funders who provide the grants to the not-for-profit organization are quite interested in how the money was spent. They can also decide a board has broken their fiduciary duty if the funds are not spent in accordance with their wishes.

I was consulting for a board that ran into some funding problems. They were building a new facility and were acting as their own contractor, which turned out to be the mistake. The project ran over in both time and in cost. The board had secured a grant that could only be received after the money was spent, so they borrowed the money to pay for the construction. When they had spent the loan, they applied for the grant and received it. Unfortunately, the board then made a mistake. Instead of paying the loan with the grant money, they paid some of the contractors who were still awaiting payment. They still needed to pay more contractors to finish the building, and the entire loan was still outstanding.

The lenders had only advanced the loan because there

was a grant in place. They were now hearing that the grant had been received and spent on the increased cost of the building instead of repaying them. The board members were personally liable for the loan. They did not discharge their fiduciary duty because they took the grant money and did not pay the loan.

The other problem is that they spent money they had not raised. They acted as their own general contractor and did not control the costs. There was a happy ending to this story. After much hand-wringing and predictions of personal doom, the organization was able to get more funding and support from the community to finish the building. The board members did not end up having to pay any money personally. We had a few sessions on strategic planning and fiduciary duty. This was not an experienced board, and they made mistakes. Luckily, they were able to recover from these mistakes.

BUDGETS

Your organization should have an annual budget. A budget is a plan for how money will be spent. A carefully prepared budget provides a road map to the organization and details the objectives of the organization for the year.

If the group gets funding from a charitable foundation or a government program, then it needs to be clear how the funds will be spent. The board needs to know that the funds are being spent in accordance with the wishes of the funder. Board members get into a lot of trouble if they do not monitor how funding is spent and the management has not spent the money in accordance with their wishes. How do you know as a board member that the funding agreements are being adhered to? What have you done to satisfy yourself on these matters?

The budget is a first step. If the funder is giving your organization $10,000, then you should have a budget that shows how that $10,000 is going to be spent.

The next step is for the board to receive financial statements at their meetings that indicates how closely the actual expenses are to the budget.

In many not-for-profit organizations, they can only spend the amount of money they receive from the funder because they do not have any other sources of funding. Expense control becomes very important in this situation.

INTERNAL CONTROL

I am sure you have heard about organizations who have been ripped off by their employees. A part of your fiduciary duty is ensuring that this is not happening in your organization. How do you do this?

Auditors

Does your organization have an auditor? If so, a part of that auditor's job is to evaluate the internal controls in your organization and evaluate the risk of fraud. Your auditor will give you some best practices to help safeguard your assets. For example, an auditor will recommend that two people authorize every expenditure made by the organization. We used to say you needed two cheque signers, but there are many more ways to pay bills now.

A board member is entitled to rely on the experts they hire, such as their auditor. It is important to ask whether the auditor has any recommendations for improving the internal controls of your organization. Once again, we are speaking of due diligence, and as we saw in chapter 2 on the duty of care, the board is allowed to rely on management and experts. But, when do you stop relying on management? If a board continues to rely on management after they have become unreliable, then a reasonable person might conclude that the board is not satisfying their duty of care.

My book *Painless Financial Literacy* goes into more detail on these topics.

When I consult with boards, the problem they have is usually either something financial or something to do with employment, and sometimes the employment issue is causing the financial issue!

Budgets and Forecasts

The organization needs to have financial statements prepared and given to you at each board meeting. The financial statements should include a comparison of the actual expenses to the organization's budget, and a forecast, which is a prediction of where the organization will end up at the end of the year. These are two different types of documents. The budget is a tool for monitoring the organization. The forecast is a prediction of the most likely set of events for the year.

They are both important, but the forecast can include items that were not predicted when the budget was prepared. The budget for example might include funding that ended up not being received, so adjustments need to be made in the forecast. Most groups will have to cut back spending if funding is reduced.

The COVID-19 pandemic caused most groups to change their predictions for the year. No one had predicted a pandemic when they were doing their 2020 budget in 2019.

Financial Statements

Your fiduciary duty extends to being able to understand financial statements. I am talking about the balance sheet, income statement, and cash flow statement that is provided at each meeting. Many people have trouble understanding the information provided. Do not be afraid to ask questions. I see many board members who think everyone understands more than they do about financial matters. If you have a question, then it is quite likely that others also have questions, and they will be relieved when you ask.

A basic understanding of financial stuff will come to you with practice. Many organizations will do some training with their directors to enable them to improve their skills in this area.

My book *Painless Financial Literacy* could help! I am sure you would enjoy reading it to improve your knowledge of the financial aspects of being a board member.

TAX ISSUES

In addition to understanding financial matters, a board member should understand the tax implications that affect not-for-profit organizations.

If the organization has employees, then they must send in the source deductions on time to avoid interest and penalties.

Board members should take steps to make sure they understand any sales tax obligations or opportunities for refunds.

In Canada, a not-for-profit organization can be eligible for a refund of 50 percent of the HST they are paying. It is also possible that a not-for-profit organization will be required to collect HST if they are operating a commercial activity such as a restaurant. These topics are beyond the scope of this book, but you can ask your organization for details on their tax framework.

FUNDING AGREEMENTS

Unsurprisingly, funders will insist on their money being spent in accordance with the funding agreement itself.

Board members are responsible for checking that the funding is actually being used the way in which it was intended. The way to do that, of course is to understand what is in the funding agreement (duty of knowledge). Board members should also ask for and understand the financial statement that compares the money spent to date on the project being funded, with the budget for the project. Every funded project should have a budget that ties into the funding agreement.

There have been cases in which management used money in ways the funding agreement did not allow. The funders would have asked where the board was when this misappropriation was going on.

This is a good question. The board has an obligation to supervise management and to be sure that all the rules are being followed.

CHAPTER SEVEN
Duty of Management

The duty of management can be a little confusing to explain.

The board should not take the role of management in the organization. What should be clear is that the board has to make sure management is taking place, but they should not be the ones who are doing the managing.

For example, the board is responsible for making sure the phones get answered by hiring and supervising the performance of staff. The board doesn't answer the phones themselves.

UNDERSTAND THE BOARD MEMBER'S ROLE

A board of directors is responsible for setting the strategic direction of the group, and management is responsible for implementing this strategy. These are the dividing lines, but there must be a balance struck. Management is often able to suggest options for the board when implementing the strategic plan.

If the executive director is experienced and long serving in the organization, then she will have valuable feedback to give to the board. The board may listen to her suggestions and decide to implement them. This does not change the board's responsibility for setting the strategic direction.

It should always be clear that the executive director reports to the board and not that the board works for the executive director. I see confusion happening when the executive director is active in assisting with finding board members. This can lead to a board member thinking they serve at the pleasure of the executive director.

Years ago, I heard tell of an organization where the board members were not brave and the executive director was involved in criminal activity. Allegedly, at some of the board meetings, a board member would ask a question about some activity that did not make sense to them, and the executive director would respond by telling the board member they did not know what they were talking about. An example of the kind of thing that happened follows.

Board member, "I don't understand why we are using grant money we received for County A to pay for a consulting project in County B. That does not seem right to me."

Executive director, "That is the way it is done in the real world. We get grant money and we can use it for whatever we want. The funding agencies don't care about what actually happens as long as we send them some kind of report."

Board member, "I don't think that could be true."

Executive director, "You don't know what you are talking about, I have been doing this the same way for years. I have more experience in this than you do."

This story came out in the open because the grant-giving organizations considered this behaviour to be misuse of funds and a breach of the board's fiduciary duty. The media questioned the board and where it was while the executive director was doing this.

In this case, the board was afraid of the executive director and had failed in their duty to manage by not effectively supervising the executive director. There are other learning points in this story as well.

Board members have to be brave, and there should be no disrespectful conversation at the boardroom table. The chair of the meeting should never have allowed the executive director to intimidate a board member at a meeting. The phrase "you don't know what you are talking about" is not respectful and is not a debate about the issues. That type of comment is a personal attack and should not be permitted.

The end of the story was that the executive director was convicted of fraud, and the organization ceased to exist. The board members were widely criticized for their failure to manage the organization properly.

BALANCING THE ROLES

There will be executive directors who act like the board is not relevant to them; they treat the organization as though they owned it. There will also be board members who think they are running the organization and do not need management. The balance you are looking for is between these extremes.

Employees

You want to have a communication channel in case an employee wants to let the board know what is going on. It is possible, in my story above, that if the employees were also not afraid of the executive director, they might have let the board know about the funds being used in the wrong manner, and the board could have dealt with that much earlier.

Whistle-Blowers

Does your organization need to set up a whistle-blower function? Is there some way to let the employees and other stakeholders know that if they see any wrong doing they should let someone know?

Small organizations will not have the resources to set up an actual hotline, but a trusted stakeholder should be found who can be contacted by anyone with something to report. The person in charge of receiving complaints needs to be someone who is not involved day-to-day with the organization; it needs to be someone who is seen as independent by those who might want to complain.

The legal counsel for the group might work in that position. The auditor of the organization is another possibility. Once someone is chosen, then you need to advertise this to those who will need to know. Put the name and contact information in the employee handbook and inform the board members in case they need to report something about the chair of the board.

Recruiting Board Members

The nomination committee has the primary responsibility for finding new board members.

Most organizations develop a policy on term limits. A term limit is what it sounds like: a limit on how long a person can be a member of a board. Best practice is such that a person stays in a position for no more than three terms of three years each. Board renewal is important if an organization is going to continue to meet new challenges. Having the same group of people run an organization for years means that nothing changes.

The nomination committee will generate a document that indicates when each of the current board members will be leaving the board based on when their terms will require them to leave the board. Generating this list is the simplest part of this role!

The board members being recruited must also have the

necessary skills. If the person leaving the board was the board member who had the in-depth financial knowledge, then they must be replaced by a board member who also has deep financial knowledge.

The nominating committee keeps track of the skills needed on the board and makes sure all the skills are represented on the board at all times.

ATTENDANCE

The nominating committee keeps track of board attendance. Most organizations have policies about missed meetings. If too many meetings are missed, then that board member will be asked to leave the board. Of course, the nominating committee has to know how many meetings each board member has missed.

The nominating committee is in charge of attendance because they are the ones tasked with replacing the board members who are asked to leave and, in most cases, they are the group that found the board members to begin with.

Potential board members will want to know how much time is needed for the position. How many meetings are there in a year? Are there other events that a board member is expected to attend? How about committees? Are the board members expected to do fund raising?

If a board appointment requires a lot of time, it will be

harder to find volunteers for the board position. It is best to be honest about this. If you get a board member to agree to serve under false pretenses, they may not stay on the board, and the recruiting effort will have been wasted.

The existing board members could be asked to keep track of the time they spend on preparing for board meetings and other board business. As an accountant, I find it quite natural to track my time each day and how it is spent, but others may not find this to be an easy task.

BOARD DISCIPLINE

The nominating committee monitors not only the attendance but also the behaviour of the board. Board members should sign annual confirmations that they are in compliance with the conflict-of-interest and confidentiality standards.

If it is determined a board member has breached confidentiality or is in a conflict-of-interest position, then an investigation might be needed. It must be determined whether the non-compliance has actually taken place. In some instances, the board member will simply admit they are at fault. In other instances, there may need to be interviews held with the board member and with those who accuse them of breaking the rules.

Board members are also responsible for upholding the code of ethics. If the code of ethics states that board members must demonstrate the values of integrity and a board member is charged with fraud, then the nominating committee will need to spring into action. Typical policies will call for a board member to be suspended from the board until the trial. If the board member is found to be innocent, then their board membership will be restored. A fraud conviction would preclude membership on most boards.

CHAPTER EIGHT
Directors' Rights

Board members also have rights. It often seems as if all we want from board members is to tell them about their obligations and all the ways they could get in trouble. Here, finally, is a chapter about the rights that only directors enjoy.

ABILITY TO VOTE

Board members are elected at the annual general meeting (AGM) of the organization. This is the last opportunity of the year for the members to vote. The rest of the meetings held in the year will be board member meetings.

The board meetings are the way in which the organization moves ahead. The board meets, makes decisions that are written in the minutes, and then management implements these decisions. As you can see, the ability to vote allows a board member to influence the direction the organization is moving in.

The ability to vote at board meetings is the best right a director has, and it is exclusive to the board members.

Notice of Meetings

Board members must be notified when a board meeting is taking place. In fact, many groups' bylaws require the notification to take place a set number of days before the meeting, often as many as thirty days before the meeting.

As a board member, know that the rest of the board cannot hold a board meeting without advising you that they are having a meeting.

Impromptu Meetings

Because of the rule that board meetings cannot take place without notice, board members should not gather in parking lots or coffee shops unless they have invited everyone. This is a tough concept to get across sometimes. Board members seem to like to talk about board business when they run into a fellow board member – at the grocery store or the gas station. These impromptu meetings are not allowed, because not every board member has been invited.

If you show up at a board meeting and realize that everyone else seems to know more about this than you do, it is possible they have had meetings to which you were not invited. Maybe not on purpose. The others may spend more time together playing golf or tennis, and maybe they discuss the issues facing the board while they are playing, which of course they should not do.

It is also possible that the group has cliques – subgroups of your group that meet on purpose to talk about the issues facing the group. This is also not allowed. In political circles, the actual meetings are more like theatre, because a lot of the decisions and voting have been worked out ahead of time as individual group members consult each other and make their plans. That is politics.

A not-for-profit board should operate in a more transparent fashion. All the board members should be at the meetings, and there should not be cliques.

ACCESS TO MANAGEMENT

A board member is entitled to reasonable access to management. How you define reasonable access will vary from group to group. The board is not to do the work of running the organization. So, they do not need to be talking to management all the time.

The executive director reports to the entire board, not an individual director. There is little reason for a board member to be visiting the executive director to issue orders.

I have worked with boards where a director thought that he should have an office at the organization, that the board members should be on site, supervising and participating in the daily operations of the organization. This is not the role of the directors. Chapter 7 on the duty of management speaks about the balance between the roles played by management and board members.

ACCESS TO GOVERNANCE DOCUMENTS

A board member is entitled to answers to their governance questions. If they would like to hear more about any of the rules in the original incorporating documents, then they can ask and should be given the information they are looking for, within a reasonable time period.

CHAPTER NINE
Board Training

As a volunteer on a board, you are donating your time because you have an interest in what is being done by this organization. You are there to help. You do not expect to become liable for any action that might be taken by the board. Governance training helps you to avoid making the kinds of mistakes that get volunteers into trouble.

I have seen a group hand a new board member a thick binder of policies and suggest that if they have any questions that they reach out to a committee member. This is unlikely to be effective. A policy manual that runs to a couple of hundred pages is going to take some time to read, and the material is not always riveting, to say the least. A board member may not read it all, and even if they do read it, will they understand the material?

Organizations should plan for how they schedule board training and how often. If a group has a lot of policies that board members need to be aware of, then more training will be needed.

Board training can be held in a variety of ways. Board

members can read policy manuals on their own (not recommended!), attend in-person training, or use on-demand training.

Some organizations have had good success with on-demand training. This might include a combination of videos and maybe a few questions being answered. Participants find this type of training more engaging than independent reading, and less engaging than the in-person training, but you cannot always schedule a governance training session for just one board member.

If you are looking for training I would like to take this opportunity to mention that I don't just write books. I offer both in-person and on-demand training (BasicBoardGovernance.ca). The in-person training can be customized to your group. The on-demand training is ready to go, right now.

If you keep track of which topics have been covered in board training and when that happened, you are able to determine whether it has been two years since the board talked about confidentiality, for example. Then it would be time to have that topic discussed during a training session.

In addition to understanding policies and governance, many organizations will do some training with their directors to enable them to improve their financial skills. A basic understanding of financial stuff will come to you with practice.

If you are not comfortable with the financial information that comes your way as a board member, then additional training is in order. Most groups will have access to someone who can explain financial concepts to you, and financial statement courses are available on line and in person.

A schedule of board training should be maintained. There is no shortage of policies that board members need to understand. Sometimes it is a better idea to have an hour of training as a part of a regular board meeting so you do not have to schedule additional meetings.

CHAPTER TEN
Insurance

Before you agree to serve on a board, be sure you ask questions about their insurance. A board member should know what is covered by the insurance purchased by the board, both for their own activities and to cover the activities of staff or various weather events that could impact the organization.

There may be insurance available for all the threats that are identified when the board does a risk assessment. If insurance is not available, then the board should be aware that they are carrying out activities that are not insured, which means that the assets of the organization are at risk.

Here are some of the usual instances where you might think about insurance.

Directors' Insurance

This insurance protects the board from any mistakes they might make. You will want to understand what is covered.

Event Insurance

No event should be held without event insurance. Contacting an insurance company and asking about obtaining insurance for the event will provide you with some additional information. It is possible the insurance company has a checklist of items that will be necessary to complete for them to offer the insurance. For example, if you are serving food, it must be prepared in a commercial kitchen by people who have taken the food handling course. It is also possible that the insurance company will not be interested in insuring the event, which should give the board pause. What are the risks of holding the event without insurance?

Professional Liability Insurance

When I serve on a board, I carry my own liability insurance. My professional liability insurance – that I am required to carry to keep my licence to practice – has a rider for each organization whose board I am serving on. I pay extra for this coverage and I think it is worth it. Do you need to obtain professional liability insurance?

Property Insurance

There are risks that exist when the organization owns property. The owner of land is the person responsible for anything that happens on that land. For example, if an oil spill contaminates land, it has to be "remediated," which costs money, often a lot of money. If the insurance for the organization is not sufficient to pay for the remediation, then the department of environment will probably levy a fine. The fine may have to be paid by the directors if the organization cannot raise the funds.

Black Swan Events

We refer to a threat no one could see coming as a Black Swan. The board has the responsibility to watch out for threats and to be as prepared as possible for any credible threat. Some of that preparation includes having insurance – very useful for mitigating the natural disaster section of the threat profile.

CHAPTER ELEVEN
To Summarize ...
Staying Out of Trouble

Staying out of trouble can be optimized by the examining the characteristics of the organization and its board meetings and then by examining yourself.

PROTECTION FOR BOARD MEMBERS

Board members often have this question. If I join a board, how will I protect myself? Some actions you can take include the following: going to the meetings, understanding financial matters, and making sure the organization is following all the rules that apply to them.

Choose the Organization

The first criteria would be to choose the organization wisely. Before you agree to serve on a board, be sure you ask questions about whether they have board insurance, whether they are being sued, and whether they are non-compliant with any government requirements.

Ask for the contact information for a few former board members. Contact them to find out why they left the board and what they can tell you about the risks of being on this particular board. These people still have a duty to keep confidential matters confidential, but they can tell you if the reason they left was because they were not comfortable with the amount of personal risk they were facing.

Attend the Meetings and Pay Attention

Make sure you attend the meetings. If you are at the meeting, then you have a chance to influence the decision being made and you also have some idea of what is going on with the organization.

If there is some decision made by the board that you absolutely cannot live with, then you resign. Once you have resigned, you are only responsible for things that happened while you were on the board.

Of course, when you attend a meeting, you should not play the role of a statue. A good board member will ask questions when they do not understand something, and they are not afraid to politely state their point of view.

Understand Financial Matters

Make sure you understand financial matters. Being able to read the financial statements and the budgets will go a long way to understanding what is going on in the organization and help you to avoid problems.

Not understanding financial information does not mean you are not responsible for financial problems that arise at the organization.

If you are not comfortable with the financial information that comes your way as a board member, then additional training is in order. Most groups will have access to someone who can explain financial concepts to you, and financial statement courses are available on line and in person.

Prepare for Meetings

Many groups send out a board package in preparation for meetings. This package includes information to be reviewed at the meeting. Board members are responsible for reviewing this information before the meeting. After this review, you may have questions to raise at the meeting.

Understand the Role of the Board

A board member should have a good understanding of the difference between a board member, a member of the organization, and management and staff.

A board member should also have a good understanding of what the board is allowed to do and what it isn't. If, for example, the incorporating documents prohibit a group from owning real property or borrowing money, then the board members should all know this. Making good decision involves understanding all the facts.

A board member should also know what is covered by the insurance purchased by the board, both for their own activities and to cover the activities of staff or various weather events that could impact the organization.

CHARACTERISTICS OF BOARD MEMBERS

Good board members tend to stay out of trouble. A good board member will have the following key characteristics: easy-going, brave, open-minded, punctual, energetic, discreet, and hard working. Of course, not everyone is perfect, but we can strive toward perfection.

Plays Well with Others

Not everyone wants to be a part of a group. I personally do not mind being a part of a group as long as I am the one in charge. So, I am not a good choice for some not-for-profit work.

The members you have who like to work together are very valuable. Part of deciding to serve on a board is knowing whether you can work as part of a team. You need to have the entire board or committee agree with you on a course of action. Some people are frustrated by this, and so they are not a good choice for the board.

Brave

A board member has to be brave. Or at least brave enough to say how they really think at the boardroom table. A board member should be comfortable enough to share their opinions and not feel intimidated if others do not agree with them. Part of this is the responsibility of the person who is chairing the meetings to make the meeting a safe space for all. The board members may need training to be able to understand that someone can disagree with them, without getting their feelings hurt.

Remember, the table is where all the board members are at the same time. If you wait to state your opinion in a less threatening place such as a one-on-one conversation after the meeting, then you have missed your opportunity to talk to all the board members. Board business should not be discussed anywhere other than the board meeting.

Open-Minded

If a board member is to be effective, they must be able to listen to different viewpoints and decide what they think is the best option to endorse. People who make their minds up and then are unable to change their minds when new information comes to light are not useful on a board.

The world appears to be getting more divisive, and we see this in politics, very clearly. The American system appears to require people from different parties to disagree, and they don't seem open to changing their minds.

I once dealt with a dysfunctional board. There were two

people on the board who disliked each other intensely. I will call them Bob and John. If Bob was in favour of a motion, then John was opposed, regardless of the issue. This made it difficult for others to come to the best decision. In fact, the correct course of action would have been to remove both members from the board, as they did not meet the criteria of having an open mind.

People are allowed to change our minds. One of the reasons meeting material is sent out well in advance of the meeting is so that the board members have time to read and consider how they feel about the decisions to be made at the meeting. There is no shame in saying you have changed your mind. In fact, admitting you were wrong about something is a sign of maturity.

Don't come to a meeting with your mind made up. Come to the meeting with some thoughts of your own and then listen to the other board members, to management, and to any experts before you decide which way you are going to vote.

Punctual

Board members should arrive at the meetings on time. This is being considerate – forcing people to wait for you before the meeting can start is not polite, obviously. Everyone is busy, but board members should be able to schedule their board commitments so they arrive on time.

Also, sometimes the entire meeting will have to wait for you because they need you for quorum.

Energetic

A board for a not-for-profit organization will often have meetings after work. Some of these meetings might take a long time, and the board member needs to have enough energy to contribute to the board meetings. Falling asleep at a board meeting is an indication that the board member does not have enough energy to serve on this board.

There may be other work to be done. Board members need to have the energy to not only read board materials but also to attend other functions or do some fundraising. If there are functions to be performed, it would be best if the board member has the energy to get them done.

Discreet

Board members are not supposed to come home after a meeting and tell their spouse everything that happened at the meeting. Telling people about how annoying some of the board members are in your group is contrary to your duty of loyalty.

People who need to talk about stuff like that are gossips. And it would be better if there were no gossips on the board.

Hard Working

Board members have a duty of diligence, which generally means that they are expected to do something. Coming to a meeting is not the only activity. One has to prepare for the meeting by reading all the information. Make sure you understand the time commitment for any board responsibilities that you take on.

This chapter explained the characteristics of perfect board members. All these traits are desirable, and you should strive to find people who will meet as many of these criteria as possible. However, no group is going to find twelve perfect board members. We are all trying to do the best we can with the people who are willing to be on your board.

GLOSSARY

Agenda – a plan for the meeting
   The agenda could be a standard listing of all the items to be discussed at a board meeting, which will be the same each time. An agenda could be a list of the decisions to be made.

Annual general meeting – the annual meeting of members
   The members elect the board, approve the annual financial statements, and appoint an auditor at this meeting.

Board – a short form of "board of directors," "board of governors," and so forth
   A board is elected by the members at the annual general meeting to oversee the running of the organization.

Board package (meeting package) – the information circulated prior to any meeting
   The board members will read this prior to the meeting taking place.

Chair – the person at the meeting who leads the discussion
   The chair is responsible for keeping the meeting on schedule and compliant with the rules.

Committee – a group with a specific task who meet and report to the board

> Typical examples include the audit committee, the finance committee, or the human resource committee.

Majority – the percentage of the votes needed to be in favour of a motion for it to be approved

> This figure is usually more than 50 percent of the participants.

Meeting – a group of people (more than one) gathering to make decisions

> The meeting can be as formal as the board meeting of a corporation or as casual as two people deciding about lunch.

Meeting package (board package) – the information circulated prior to any meeting

> The board members will read this prior to the meeting taking place.

Member – a person who has privileges because of joining an organization

Minutes – a record of what was accomplished at the meeting

> This can be a written record or audio and video recordings.

Motions – decisions voted on by the group, may also be called resolutions.
Motion passed – a motion gets more votes (a majority) in favour than not.
Motion defeated – a motion fails to get enough votes. This means that whatever was being moved is not going to happen.
Motion tabled – a motion is deferred to the next meeting or to a meeting in the future. Typically, this is done when the group wants more time to make the decision.

Participant – a person attending a meeting who can vote

Quorum – the minimum number of participants required to be present at a meeting before the meeting can make any decisions

Risk assessments – consideration of all the things that could possibly go wrong

Skill matrix – a document showing all the skills that are needed on the board
For example, an organization may need someone with financial skills, legal skills, or human resource skills.

Tabled – a motion is deferred to the next meeting or to a meeting in the future
Typically, this is done when the group wants more time to make the decision.

OTHER BOOKS BY DEBI J. PEVERILL

Basic Board Governance

Budgeting Essentials

Can Your Business Be Sold?

Every Canadian's Guide to Financial Prosperity

Painless Financial Literacy

Starting a Successful Business

Taxation Adventures

Ten Tax Traps to Avoid

Effective Meetings Series

How to Craft an Effective Agenda

How to Chair an Effective Meeting

How to Take Minutes Effectively

Effective Meetings: Complete Series

ABOUT THE AUTHOR

Debi J. Peverill has attended thousands of meetings during her decades-long career as a Chartered Professional Accountant and a professional speaker.

Debi is a rare individual: an accountant with a sense of humour and no fear of public speaking. She has a particular interest in governance, taxation, and financial management.

Debi teaches courses in the Sobeys School of Business at Saint Mary's University, Halifax; runs her public accounting practice; and finds time to record helpful tips on LinkedIn, Twitter, and YouTube twice a week. She also writes on Medium and her own blog at DebiPeverill.ca.

She is the mother of two grown children and lives with her long-suffering husband in Lower Sackville, Nova Scotia.

FOR MORE INFORMATION

- X (formerly Twitter): @DebiPev

- LinkedIn.com/in/DebiPeverill

- YouTube.com/c/DebiPeverillPFTG

- DebiPev.Medium.com

- Peverill.ca (accounting business)
  DebiPeverill.ca (financial tips)
  PainlessFinancialTrainingGroup.ca (books and courses)

www.ingramcontent.com/pod-product-compliance
Lightning Source LLC
Chambersburg PA
CBHW050327230526
45471CB00005B/2392